A Quail in Jail

and

The Rain Is a Pain

Level 3 – Yellow

Helpful Hints for Reading at Home

The graphemes (written letters) and phonemes (units of sound) used throughout this series are aligned with Letters and Sounds. This offers a consistent approach to learning whether reading at home or in the classroom.

HERE IS A LIST OF PHONEMES FOR THIS PHASE OF LEARNING. AN EXAMPLE OF THE PRONUNCIATION CAN BE FOUND IN BRACKETS.

Phase 3			
j (jug)	v (van)	w (wet)	x (fox)
y (yellow)	z (zoo)	zz (buzz)	qu (quick)
ch (chip)	sh (shop)	th (thin/then)	ng (ring)
ai (rain)	ee (feet)	igh (night)	oa (boat)
oo (boot/look)	ar (farm)	or (for)	ur (hurt)
ow (cow)	oi (coin)	ear (dear)	air (fair)
ure (sure)	er (corner)		

HERE ARE SOME WORDS WHICH YOUR CHILD MAY FIND TRICKY.

Phase 3 Tricky Words			
he	you	she	they
we	all	me	are
be	my	was	her

TOP TIPS FOR HELPING YOUR CHILD TO READ:

- Allow children time to break down unfamiliar words into units of sound and then encourage children to string these sounds together to create the word.

- Encourage your child to point out any focus phonics when they are used.

- Read through the book more than once to grow confidence.

- Ask simple questions about the text to assess understanding.

- Encourage children to use illustrations as prompts.

This book focuses on the phonemes /ai/ and /ee/ and is a yellow level 3 book band.

A Quail in Jail
and
The Rain Is a Pain

Written by
Mignonne Gunasekara

Illustrated by
Amy Li

Can you say this sound and draw it with your finger?

A Quail in Jail

Written by
Mignonne Gunasekara

Illustrated by
Amy Li

A quail sits in jail. Is it a bad quail?

Did it rob the queen? No, the quail did not.

Did it wee on a leek? No, it did not.

Did the quail wail at the maid?

Did the quail set the bait and wait?

Did the quail tip the pail and get her wet?

Yes! The quail did. It is a bad, bad quail.

Is the maid well? No! She is in pain.

Is the quail well? The pail fell on its tail.

That is the deed that put the quail in jail.

The quail will not get bail.

The jail will keep the bad, bad quail.

Can you say this sound and draw it with your finger?

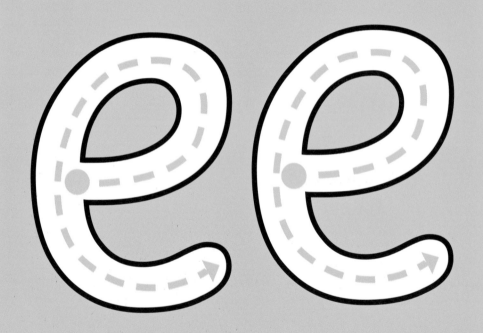

The Rain Is a Pain

Written by
Mignonne Gunasekara

Illustrated by
Amy Li

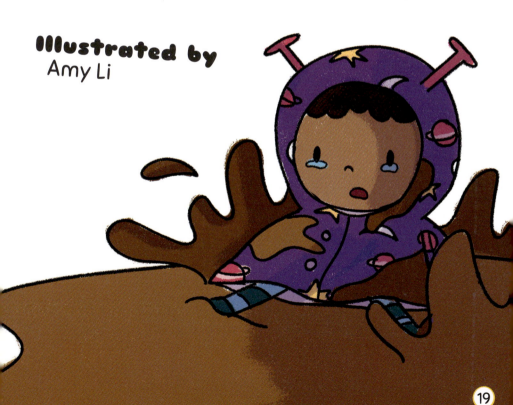

"The Sun is not up. I cannot see it."

"Let me peek… Can I see hail?"

"No. Wait! It is wet. I see the rain!"

The aim is to get the mail.

The kids are keen to hop in the mud.

"I seek fun in the mud!"
"I need to hop!"

They cannot see that the mud is deep.

Hop! They feel the wet seep in.
It seems fun…

… but it is not! The kids' feet are wet.

"Eek!" they wail. "Wet feet will reek!" they weep.

The kids fail to get the mail.

"Did you get the mail?"
"No... rain is a pain."

©2022 **BookLife Publishing Ltd.**
King's Lynn, Norfolk, PE30 4LS, UK

ISBN 978-1-80155-474-9
All rights reserved. Printed in Poland.
A catalogue record for this book is available from the British Library.

A Quail in Jail & The Rain Is a Pain
Written by Mignonne Gunasekara
Illustrated by Amy Li

An Introduction to BookLife Readers...

Our Readers have been specifically created in line with the London Institute of Education's approach to book banding and are phonetically decodable and ordered to support each phase of Letters and Sounds.

Each book has been created to provide the best possible reading and learning experience. Our aim is to share our love of books with children, providing both emerging readers and prolific page-turners with beautiful books that are guaranteed to provoke interest and learning, regardless of ability.

BOOK BAND GRADED using the Institute of Education's approach to levelling.

PHONETICALLY DECODABLE supporting each phase of Letters and Sounds.

EXERCISES AND QUESTIONS to offer reinforcement and to ascertain comprehension.

BEAUTIFULLY ILLUSTRATED to inspire and provoke engagement, providing a variety of styles for the reader to enjoy whilst reading through the series.

AUTHOR INSIGHT:
MIGNONNE GUNASEKARA

Born in Sri Lanka, Mignonne has always been drawn to stories, whether they are told through literature, film or music. After studying Biomedical Science at King's College London, Mignonne completed a short course in screenwriting at the National Centre for Writing in Norwich, during which she explored writing scripts for the different mediums of film, theatre and radio.

This book focuses on the phonemes /ai/ and /ee/ and is a yellow level 3 book band.